The Cynic's Almanac
Paul Erland

"Cynic: n., a blackguard whose faulty vision sees things as they are, not as they ought to be."
—Ambrose Bierce

© Copyright 1996 by Paul Erland. All rights reserved.

ISBN: 1-886371-26-1

Cynic's Ink
3012 Hedrick St.
Nashville, TN 37203

Cover photography and design: Mike Walker, Limbic Graphics, Nashville, Tennessee.

Introduction

Walk into any bookstore these days, and what do you see? About half an acre of "inspirational" works—volumes full of uplifting thoughts, sappy poetry, heartwarming anecdotes. Who are the best-selling non-fiction "authors?" Half-wits with a knack for sugar-coating everything, for assuring us that this is the best of all possible worlds, that man is the pinnacle of God's creation, and that each and every one of us is endowed with a touch of the Divine spark, not to mention a generous helping of genius just waiting to be tapped.

This book is an argument against these puny Panglosses, and an antidote to their sickeningly-sweet concoctions. It is a tribute to the great writers and personalities who, in spite of their peccadilloes, at least had a firm foothold in reality. It will be, I hope, inspirational in its own way, if it makes you, as it made me, think—even if you can't help thinking how lousy things are.

Have a rotten day!

Key to the Book's Format

Quotations cited were spoken by the person(s) whose date of birth or death occurred on that day, unless otherwise noted.

JANUARY

BIRTHDAY OF THE MONTH: Elvis Presley, born January 8, 1935.

Elvis Presley had nothing to do with excellence, just myth.
—Marlon Brando.

---

1 J. D. Salinger, American author, born, 1919.

What I'd do, I figured, I'd go out west where it was very pretty and sunny and where nobody knew me and I'd get a job. . .I'd pretend I was one of those deaf-mutes. That way I wouldn't have to have any goddam stupid useless conversations with anybody.
—The Catcher In The Rye

---

2 First successful heart transplant, 1968.

A man's heart is a grave long before he is buried. Youth dies, and beauty, and hope, and desire.
—Eric Hoffer.

January

3   Cicero, Roman orator, 106 B. C.

> *What orators lack in depth*
> *they make up to you in length.*
>   —Montesquieu.

4   Albert Camus, author and existentialist, dies in car crash, 1960.

> *There is no fate that cannot be surmounted by scorn.*
>   —Camus.

5   Calvin Coolidge dies, 1933.

> *Calvin Coolidge didn't say much, and when he did he didn't say much.*
>   —Will Rogers.

6   Carl Sandburg, American poet, 1878.

> *The cruellest thing that has happened to Lincoln since he was shot by Booth has been to fall into the hands of Carl Sandburg.*
>   —Edmund Wilson.

January

7 John Berryman, poet, commits suicide, 1972.

> *Amid the sufferings of life on earth,*
> *suicide is God's best gift to man.*
> —Pliny the Elder.

8 World Literacy Day.

> *Books are the curse of the human race.*
> —Benjamin Disraeli.

9 Richard Nixon born, 1913.

> *Nixon is a shifty-eyed goddam liar.*
> —Harry S Truman.

10 First session of U.N. General Assembly, 1946.

> *The world is a republic of mediocrities,*
> *and always was.*
> —Thomas Carlyle.

January

11
William James, American philosopher, born 1842.

Religion is a monumental chapter in the history of human egotism.

12
Edmund Burke, British statesman and orator, born 1729.

We have a degree of delight in the real misfortunes and pains of others.

13
Edmund Spenser, English poet, died, 1599.

Death is the end of woes.

14
Albert Schweitzer born, 1875.

High-toned humanitarians constantly overestimate the sufferings of those they sympathize with.
—H. L. Mencken.

A humanitarian is always a hypocrite.
—George Orwell.

January

15 Molière, French dramatist, born 1622.

Man, I can assure you, is a nasty creature.

16 Edward Gibbon (*The Decline and Fall of the Roman Empire*) dies, 1794.

Very few things happen at the right time and the rest do not happen at all. The conscientious historian will correct these defects.
—Herodotus.

17 Anton Chekhov, Russian writer, born 1860.

And the whole world, the whole of life, seemed to Ryabovich an unintelligible, aimless jest. . .The water was running, he knew not where or why. . .It had flowed into a great river, from the great river into the sea; then it had risen in vapor, turned into rain, and perhaps the very same water was running now before his eyes again. . .And why? For what purpose?
—The Kiss

January

18 Montesquieu, French philosopher, born 1689.

One must mourn not at the death of men, but at their birth.

19 Edgar Allen Poe born, 1809.

The play is the tragedy, "Man," and its hero the Conqueror Worm.

20 Martin Luther King, Jr. Day.

It's silly to go on pretending that under the skin we are all brothers. The truth is more likely that under the skin we are all cannibals, assassins, traitors, liars, hypocrites, poltroons.
—Henry Miller.

21 George Orwell (1984) dies, 1950.

If you want a picture of the future, imagine a boot stomping on the human face—forever.

January

22 Francis Bacon, English philosopher and essayist, born 1561.

The world's a bubble; and the life of man less than a span.

23 Stendhal, French novelist, born 1783.

Love as it exists in high society is a love of duelling and a love of gambling.

24 Oral Roberts born, 1918.

Man is certainly stark mad. He cannot make a worm, and yet he will be making gods by dozens.
—Montaigne.

25 Somerset Maugham, British author, born 1874.

People ask you for criticism, but they only want praise.

January

26 Douglas MacArthur born, 1880.

> *Oh yes, I studied dramatics under him for twelve years.*
> —Dwight D. Eisenhower.

27 Lewis Carroll born, 1832.

> *"If everybody minded their own business," said the Duchess in a hoarse growl, "the world would go round a deal faster than it does."*
> —Alice In Wonderland

28 William B. Yeats, poet, dies, 1939.

> *(His epitaph, self-composed:*
> *Cast a cold eye*
> *On life, on death.*
> *Horseman, Pass by.)*
>
> *All life weighed in the scales of my own life seems to me to be a preparation for something that never happens.*

January

29 H. L. Mencken dies, 1956.

When I die I shall be content to vanish into nothingness. . .no show, no matter how good, could conceivably be good forever.

---

30 Franklin Delano Roosevelt born, 1882.

No one is fit to be trusted with power. . .No one.
—C. P. Snow.

---

31 Norman Mailer born, 1923.

Once a newspaper touches a story, the facts are lost forever, even to the protagonists.

FEBRUARY

BIRTHDAY OF THE MONTH: Ronald Reagan, born February 6, 1911.

Ronald Reagan is a triumph of the embalmer's art.
                                                      —Gore Vidal.

1 Langston Hughes, American black poet, born 1902.

I swear to the Lord
I still can't see
Why democracy means
Everybody but me.

2 James Joyce, Irish writer, born 1882.

My God, what a clumsy olla putrida...Nothing but old fags and cabbage stumps of quotations from the Bible and the rest, stewed in the juice of deliberate, journalistic dirty-mindedness.
—D. H. Lawrence, referring to *Ulysses.*

February

3 Gertrude Stein, American writer, born 1874.

Miss Stein was a past master in making nothing happen very slowly.
—Clifton Fadiman.

4 Liberace dies, 1987.

Those who make their dress a principal part of themselves will, in general, become of no more value than their dress.
—William Hazlitt.

5 Thomas Carlyle, English essayist, dies, 1881.

O poor mortals, how ye make this earth bitter for each other.

6 Babe Ruth born, 1896.

It's [baseball] a business, I tell you. There ain't no sentiment to it. Forget that stuff.

February

7
Charles Dickens born, 1812.

Against the disease of writing one must take special precautions, since it is a dangerous and contagious disease.
—Pierre Abelard.

8
John Ruskin, English author, born 1819.

We call ourselves a rich nation, and we are filthy and foolish enough to thumb each other's books out of circulating libraries!

9
George Ade, American humorist, born 1866.

It isn't how long you stick around but how much you put over while you are here.

10
Boris Pasternak (*Dr. Zhivago*), born 1890.

The great majority of us are required to live a life of constant duplicity.

February

11 Thomas Edison born, 1847.

We don't know a millionth of one percent about anything.

12 Charles Darwin born, 1809.

Perhaps the most admirable among the admirable laws of Nature is the survival of the weakest.
—Vladimir Nabokov.

13 First magazine published in U.S., 1741.

I see no point in reading.
—Louis XIV.

14 Valentine's Day.

To be in love is merely to be in a state of perpetual anaesthesia.
—H. L. Mencken.

February

15 John Barrymore, American actor, born 1882.

The good die young because they see it's no use living if you've got to be good.

16 Henry Adams, American historian, born 1838.

One friend in a lifetime is much; two are many; three are hardly possible.

17 Heinrich Heine, German poet and writer, dies, 1856.

Sleep is lovely, death is better still, not to have been born is of course the miracle.

18 Nikos Kazantzakis, Greek philosopher and writer, born 1883.

Never trust a Greek.
—Euripides.

February

19 Edison granted patent on phonograph, 1878.

Dear Mr. Edison: I am astonished and terrified at the results of this evening's experiment. Astonished at the wonderful form you have developed and terrified at the thought that so much hideous and bad music will be put on records forever.
—Sir Arthur Sullivan.

20 U. S. Post Office established, 1792.

I have received no more than one or two letters that were worth the postage.
—Henry David Thoreau.

21 W. H. Auden, poet, born 1907.

The high-water mark, so to speak, of Socialist literature, is W. H. Auden, a sort of gutless Kipling.
—George Orwell.

He was a dictatorial bastard. He was a tyrant.
—Truman Capote.

February

22 Edna St. Vincent Millay, poet, born 1892.

It is not true that life is one damned thing after another—it is one damn thing over and over.

23 Samuel Pepys, English diarist, born 1633.

Strange to say what delight we married people have to see these poor fools decoyed into our condition.

24 George Moore, English philosopher, born 1852.

Humanity is a pigsty where liars, hypocrites and the obscene in spirit congregate.

25 Tennessee Williams, playwright, dies, 1983.

A man, when he burns, leaves only a handful of ashes. No woman can hold him. The wind must blow him away.

February

26 Victor Hugo, French author, born 1802.

A glittering humbug.
—Thomas Carlyle.

27 Elizabeth Taylor born, 1932.

Remember that the most beautiful things in the world are the most useless; peacocks and lilies for example.
—John Ruskin.

28 Montaigne, French philosopher and essayist, born 1533.

The ceaseless labor of a man's whole life is to build the house of death.

MARCH

BIRTHDAY OF THE MONTH: Alexander Graham Bell, born March 3, 1847; Bell patented the telephone, March 7, 1876.

O misery, misery, mumble and moan!
Someone invented the telephone,
And interrupted a nation's slumbers,
Ringing wrong but similar numbers.
—Ogden Nash

1 Lytton Strachey, English biographer, born 1880.

The horror of getting up is unparalleled,
and I am filled with amazement every morning
when I find that I have done it.

2 Horace Walpole, English author and wit, dies, 1797.

The world is a comedy to those that think,
a tragedy to those that feel.

March

3 Jean Harlow, American actress ("The Blonde Bombshell"), born 1911.

It isn't that gentlemen really prefer blondes it's just that we look dumber.
—Anita Loos.

4 Charles Goren, bridge expert, born 1901.

Bridge I regard as only one degree better than absolutely vacuous conversation.
—A.C. Benson.

5 Rex Harrison, actor, born 1908.

What a set of barren asses are actors.
—John Keats.

6 Ring Lardner, American humorist, born 1885.

You know what Barnum said. Well, he didn't go far enough. They like to be bunked, but what they like most of all is to bunk themselves.

March

7   U. S. Constitution went into effect, 1789.

That all men are equal is a proposition to which. . .no sane individual has ever given his assent.
—Aldous Huxley.

8   International Women's Day.

Women should remain at home, sit still, keep house, and bear and bring up children.
—Martin Luther

9   Bobby Fischer, chess champion, born 1943.

Chess is the greatest waste of human intelligence that can be found outside of an advertising agency.
—Raymond Chandler.

10   James Herriott born, 1916. (*All Things Bright and Beautiful.*)

I loathe people who keep dogs. They are cowards who haven't got the guts to bite people themselves.
—August Strindberg.

March

11 First publicly played basketball game, 1892.

Nothing here but basketball, a game which won't be fit for people until they set the basket umbilicus-high and return the giraffes to the zoo.
　　　　　　　　　　—Ogden Nash.

12 Jack Kerouac, American writer, born 1922.

That's not writing, that's typing.
　　　　　—Truman Capote
　　　　on Kerouac's novel,
　　　　On The Road.

13 Clarence Darrow, American trial lawyer, dies, 1938.

I think we may class the lawyer in the natural history of monsters.
　　　　　　　—John Keats.

March

14 Albert Einstein born, 1879.

I have never met a man yet who understands in the least what Einstein is driving at. . .I very seriously doubt that Einstein himself knows what he is driving at.
—William Henry Cardinal O'Connor.

15 Andrew Jackson born, 1767.

One of the most unfit men I know of for such a place.
(*The Presidency*) Thomas Jefferson.

16 West Point established, 1802.

The professional military mind is by necessity an inferior and unimaginative mind; no man of high intellectual quality would willingly imprison his gifts in such a calling.
—H. G. Wells.

17 St. Patrick dies, 461.

Saint, n. A dead sinner revised and edited.
—Ambrose Bierce.

March

18 John Updike, American author, born 1932.

> I hate him. Everything about him bores me.
> —Truman Capote.

19 Sir Richard Burton, explorer and author, born 1821.

> There is no Heaven, there is no Hell;
> these be the dreams of baby minds.

20 Henrik Ibsen, Norwegian dramatist, born 1828.

> The public doesn't require any new ideas. The public is best served by the good, old-fashioned ideas it already has.

21 Johann S. Bach, born 1685.

> Classical music is the kind we keep hoping will turn into a tune.
> —Kin Hubbard.

March

22 Marcel Marceau, mime, born 1923.

I do not get my ideas from people on the street. If you look at faces on the street, what do you see? Nothing. Just boredom.

23 Fanny Farmer, cookbook author, born 1857.

God sends meat and the Devil sends cooks.
—English proverb.

24 Longfellow dies, 1882.

*And our hearts, like muffled
Drums, are beating funeral marches
 to the grave.*

25 Flannery O'Connor, American author, born 1925.

*"Shut up, Bobby Lee," the Misfit said.
"It's no real pleasure in life."*
—A Good Man Is Hard to Find

March

26 A. E. Housman, English poet, born 1859.

> *Eyes the shady night have shut*
> *Cannot see the record cut;*
> *And silence is no worse than cheers*
> *After earth has stopped the ears.*
> —To An Athlete Dying Young

27 U. S. Navy established, 1794.

> *Military men are the scourges of the world.*
> —Guy de Maupassant.

28 Virginia Woolf, American writer, dies, 1941.

Life. . .is arduous, difficult, a perpetual struggle. It calls for gigantic courage and strength. . .and how can we generate this. . .? By thinking that other people are inferior to oneself.

March

29 Beethoven gives first public performance in Vienna, 1795.

Beethoven always sounded to me like the upsetting of bags of nails, with here and there an also dropped hammer.
—John Ruskin.

30 Vincent Van Gogh born, 1853.

I believe more and more that God must not be judged on this earth. It is one of his sketches that has turned out badly.

31 René Descartes, French philosopher ("I think, therefore I am."), born, 1596.

Most people would sooner die than think; in fact, they do so.
—Bertrand Russell.

APRIL

BIRTHDAY OF THE MONTH: W. C. Fields, April 9, 1880.

I am free of all prejudices. I hate everyone equally.

1 April Fools' Day.

Hain't we got all the fools in town on our side? And hain't that a big enough majority in any town?
—Mark Twain, Huckleberry Finn.

2 Charlemagne born, 743.

Kings are not born: they are made by universal hallucination.
—George Bernard Shaw.

3 Doris Day born, 1924.

Personality untouched by human emotions, her brow unclouded by human thought, her form unsmudged by the slightest evidence of femininity.
—John Simon.

April

4   Martin Luther King, Jr. killed, 1968.

The brotherhood of man is not a mere poet's dream; it is a most depressing and humiliating reality.
—Oscar Wilde.

5   Thomas Hobbes, English philosopher, born 1588.

The condition of man is a condition of war of everyone against everyone.

6   Lincoln Steffens, American author, born 1866.

Power is what men seek, and any group that gets it will abuse it. It is the same old story.

7   Willaim Wordsworth, poet, born 1770.

*Have I not reason to lament
What man has made of man?*

April

8 Buddha, born 563 B. C. (?)

Man prefers to believe what he prefers to be true.

9 Hugh Hefner born, 1926.

Not a shred of evidence exists in favor of the idea that life is serious.
—Brendan Gill.

10 Evelyn Waugh, English writer, born 1903.

If politicians and scientists were lazier, how much happier we should all be.

11 Leo Rosten, American humorist, born 1908.

I never cease being dumfounded by the unbelievable things people believe.

April

12 Civil War begins, 1861.

There they are cutting each other's throats, because one half of them prefer having their servants for life, and the other by the hour.
—Thomas Carlyle.

13 Samuel Beckett, Irish poet and playwright, born 1906.

It (Waiting for Godot) is pretentious gibberish, without any claim to importance whatsoever. . .It's just a waste of everybody's time and it makes me ashamed to think that such balls could be taken seriously for a moment.
—Noel Coward.

14 Income taxes due tomorrow!

Wherever a man goes, men will pursue him and paw him with their dirty institutions.
—Thoreau.

April

15 Henry James born, 1843.

Henry James wrote fiction as if it were a painful duty.
—Oscar Wilde.

16 Charlie Chaplin born, 1889.

The son of a bitch is a ballet dancer.
—W. C. Fields.

17 Thornton Wilder, American author, born 1897.

The public for which masterpieces are intended is not on this earth.

18 Clarence Darrow born, 1857.

Lawyers are always more ready to get a man into troubles than out of them.
—Oliver Goldsmith.

April

19 Lord Byron dies, 1824.

I will have nothing to do with your immortality; we are miserable enough in this life.

20 Adolf Hitler born, 1889.

The great masses of people. . .will more easily fall victims to a grand lie than to a small one.

21 Mark Twain dies, 1910.

Whoever has lived long enough to find out what life is, knows how deep a debt of gratitude we owe to Adam, the first great benefactor of our race.
He brought death into our world.

22 Henry Fielding, English novelist, born 1707.

That monstrous animal a husband and wife.

April

23 William Shakespeare born, 1564.

> *Crude, immoral, vulgar, and senseless.*
> —Tolstoy.

---

24 Library of Congress created, 1800.

> *Every man with a belly full of the classics is an enemy of the human race.*
> —Henry Miller.

---

25 Guglielmo Marconi, inventor of radio, born, 1874.

> *Radio the triumph of illiteracy.*
> —John Dos Passos.

---

26 Daniel Defoe, English novelist, dies 1661.

> *The best of men cannot suspend their fate:*
> *The good die early and the bad die late.*

April

27 Herbert Spencer, English philosopher, born 1820.

Time: That which man is always trying to kill, but which ends in killing him.

28 Lionel Barrymore, American actor, born 1878.

Actors are crap.
—John Ford.

29 Rod McKuen, American poet, born 1933.

People do not deserve to have good writing, they are so pleased with bad.
—Emerson.

30 Joan of Arc burned at stake, 1431.

It is often pleasant to stone a martyr, no matter how much we may admire him.
—John Barth.

MAY

HOLIDAY OF THE MONTH: Mother's Day.

> *The mother cult is something that will set future generations roaring with laughter.*
> —Gustave Flaubert.

1 John Dryden, English poet laureate, dies, 1700.

> *When I consider life, 'tis all a cheat,*
> *Yet fooled with hope, men favor the deceit.*

2 Benjamin Spock, child care expert, born 1903.

> *Beat your child once a day. If you don't know why, the child does.*
> —Chinese proverb.

3 Machiavelli, Italian statesman and writer, born 1469.

> *Speaking generally, men are ungrateful, fickle, hypocritical, fearful of danger and covetous of gain.*

May

4
Academy of Motion Picture Arts and Sciences founded, 1927.

> *Movies are one of the bad habits that have corrupted our century.*
> —Ben Hecht.

5
Søren Kierkegaard, Danish philosopher, born 1813.

> *My life is absolutely meaningless.*

6
Sigmund Freud born, 1856.

> *I think he's crude, I think he's medieval, and I don't want an elderly gentleman from Vienna with an umbrella inflicting his dreams upon me.*
> —Vladimir Nabokov.

7
American Medical Association founded, 1847.

> *Doctors pour drugs of which they know little, to cure diseases of which they know less, into human beings of whom they know nothing.*
> —Voltaire.

May

8 Harry S Truman, born 1884.

I sit here all day trying to do the things they ought to have sense enough to do without my persuading them. That's all the powers of the President amount to.

9 J. M. Barrie (*Peter Pan*), born 1860.

Every man that is high up loves to think that he has done it all by himself; and the wife smiles, and lets it go at that.

10 Ariel Durant, American historian, born 1898.

It is good that a historian should remind himself, now and then, that he is a particle pontificating on infinity.

11 Stanley Elkin, American writer, born 1930.

If you can't make people miserable by writing, what's the point?

May

12 Dante Gabriel Rosetti, English poet and painter, born 1828.

*The hour when you learn that all is vain
And that Hope sows what Love shall never reap.*

13 Daphne du Maurier, English novelist (*Rebecca*), born 1907.

Writers should be read, but neither seen nor heard.

14 *Resistance to Civil Government*, by Henry David Thoreau published, 1849.

*There is no nonsense so arrant that it cannot be made
the creed of the vast majority by
adequate governmental action.*
— Bertrand Russell.

15 Emily Dickinson dies, 1886.

*Success is counted sweetest
By those who ne'er succeed.*

16 Armed Forces Day.

The existence of the soldier, next to capital punishment, is the most grievous vestige of barbarism which survives among men.
—Alfred de Vigny.

17 Benjamin Disraeli, British Prime Minister, born 1804.

It destroys one's nerves to be amiable every day to the same human being.

18 Bertrand Russell, philosopher, born 1872.

I have always thought respectable people scoundrels.

19 Boys Clubs of America founded, 1906.

Launch your boat, blessed youth, and flee at full speed from every form of culture.
—Epicurus.

May

20 First trans-Atlantic air service began, 1939.

The conquest of the air, so jubilantly hailed by general opinion, may turn out the most sinister event that ever befell us.
—John Galsworthy.

21 Alexander Pope, English poet, born 1688.

This long disease, my life.

22 Richard Wagner, German composer, born 1813.

Wagner had some wonderful moments but awful half hours.
—Rossini.

23 First cross-country automobile race, 1923.

Thanks to the Interstate Highway System, it is now possible to travel from coast to coast without seeing anything.
—Charles Kuralt.

May

24 Bob Dylan born, 1941.

*Man was never meant to sing:
And all his mimic organs e'er expressed
Was but an imitative howl at best.*
—John Langhorne.

25 Ralph Waldo Emerson born, 1803.

Society never advances.

26 Sally Ride, first U. S. woman astronaut, born 1951.

They have a right to work wherever they want to—as long as they have dinner ready when you get home.
—John Wayne, born May 26, 1907.

27 Louise-Ferdinand Celine, French writer, born 1894.

For the poor of this world, two major ways of expiring are available: either by the absolute indifference of your fellow men in peace time, or by the homicidal passion of these same when war breaks out.

May

28 Jim Thorpe, greatest American athlete ever, born 1888.

I hate all sports as rabidly as a person who likes sports hates common sense.
—H. L. Mencken.

29 G. K. Chesterton, English author, born 1874.

If a thing is worth doing, it is worth doing badly.

30 Voltaire, French philosopher, dies, 1788.

The godless arch-scoundrel! Voltaire is dead dead like a dog, like a beast.
—Mozart.

31 Walt Whitman, poet, born 1819.

Animals do not make me sick discussing their duty to God.

JUNE

HOLIDAY OF THE MONTH: Father's Day.

> *Father and son are natural enemies and each is happier and more secure in keeping it that way.*
> —John Steinbeck.

1 John Masefield, English poet laureate, born 1878.

> *Life is a long headache in a noisy street.*

2 Thomas Hardy, English novelist and poet, born 1840.

> *Nobody came, because nobody does.*
> —Jude The Obscure

3 First U. S. spacewalk, 1965.

> *Outer space is no place for a person of breeding.*
> —Lady Violet Bonham Carter.

June

4   George III, King of England, born 1738.

> *George the Third*
> *Ought never to have occurred*
> *One can only wonder*
> *At so grotesque a blunder.*
> —Edmund Clerihew Bentley.

5   Stephen Crane, American writer, dies, 1900, of tuberculosis.

> *We should weep for men at their birth,*
> *not at their death.*
> —Montesquieu.

6   Thomas Mann, German writer, born 1875.

What we call mourning for our dead is perhaps not so much grief at not being able to call them back as it is grief at not being able to want to do so.

June

7 Paul Gauguin, artist, born 1848.

Fame! What a vain word, and what a vain recompense! I only think of withdrawing myself from men, and in consequence far from fame.
—Gauguin

Don't talk to me of Gauguin. I'd like to wring the fellow's neck!
—Cézanne.

8 Joan Rivers born, 1933.

What a sad business is being funny!
—Charlie Chaplin.

9 Senior Citizens' Day, Oklahoma.

The only good thing about it (old age) is you're not dead.
—Lillian Hellman.

June

10 Alcoholics Anonymous founded, 1910.

> *I drink to make other people interesting.*
> —George Jean Nathan.

11 Saul Bellow, American writer (Nobel Prize), born 1915.

> *Saul Bellow is a nothing writer. He doesn't exist.*
> —Truman Capote.

12 Anne Frank born, 1929.

> *It is the folly of the world, constantly, which confounds its wisdom.*
> —Oliver Wendell Holmes.

13 W. B. Yeats, poet, born 1865.

> *Come away, O human child!*
> *. . . For the world's more full of weeping than you can understand.*

June

14 Flag Day.

The American people. . .constitute the most timorous, snivelling, poltroonish, ignominious mob of serfs and goosesteppers ever gathered under one flag in Christendom since the end of the Middle Ages.
—H. L. Mencken.

15 Dante Aligheri named Prior of Florence, 1300.

All right, then, I'll say it. Dante makes me sick.
—Lope de Vega, on his deathbed.

16 Joyce Carol Oates, American author, born 1938.

She's a joke monster.
—Truman Capote.

17 First commercial around-the-world flight began, 1947. Watergate scandal uncovered, 1972.

The more humanity advances,
the more it is degraded.
—Gustave Flaubert.

June

18 Paul McCartney born, 1942.

The Beatles are not merely awful...They are so unbelievably horrible, so appallingly unmusical, so dogmatically insensitive to the magic of the art, that they qualify as crowned heads of anti-music.
—William F. Buckley.

Well, you know, a lot of Americans are unbalanced.
—Paul McCartney.

19 Blaise Pascal, French philosopher and mathematician, born 1623.

We shall die alone.

20 Lillian Hellman, American author, born 1925.

Nobody outside of a baby carriage or a judge's chamber believes in an unprejudiced point of view.

June

21 Jean-Paul Sartre, French writer and existentialist, born 1905.

The world could get along very well without literature; it could get along even better without man.

22 Galileo recants, 1633.

I do not feel obliged to believe that that same God who has endowed us with sense, reason and intellect has intended us to forgo their use.
—Galileo

Coward: One who in a perilous emergency thinks with his legs.
—Ambrose Bierce.

23 Alfred Kinsey, pioneer sexual researcher, born, 1894.

There is hardly anyone whose sexual life, if it were broadcast, would not fill the world at large with surprise and horror.
—W. Somerset Maugham.

June

24
Ambrose Bierce, American author (*The Devil's Dictionary*) and noted cynic, born 1842.

Bierce would bury his best friend with a sigh of relief, and express satisfaction that he was done with him.
                              —Jack London.

25
Custer's Last Stand, 1876.

When the cavalry won it was a great victory, and when the Indians won it was a massacre.
                              —Dick Gregory.

26
Pearl Buck (*The Good Earth*), born 1892.

Anybody that could have given the Nobel Prize to Pearl Buck ought to go and be examined by a mental institution.
                              —Truman Capote.

27
Edward Gibbon completes *The History of the Decline and Fall of the Roman Empire*, 1787.

History is little more than the register of the crimes, follies and misfortunes of mankind.

June

28 World War I begins, 1914; ends same day, 1919.

You can't say civilization don't advance—in every war they kill you in a new way.
— Will Rogers.

29 Antoine de Saint-Exupéry, French aviator and writer, born 1900.

Grown-ups never understand anything for themselves, and it's tiresome for children to be always and forever explaining things to them.

30 *Gone With the Wind* published, 1936.

Frankly, my dear, I don't give a damn.
— Rhett Butler.

JULY

BIRTHDAY OF THE MONTH: Henry Ford, July 12, 1863.

I have always considered that the substitution of the internal combustion machine for the horse marked a very gloomy milestone in the progress of mankind.
—Winston Churchill.

1 George Sand, French novelist, born 1804.

I have had my bellyful of great men. . .In real life they are nasty creatures, persecutors, temperamental, despotic, bitter and suspicious.

2 Ernest Hemingway dies, 1961.

Hemingway was a jerk.
—Harold Robbins.

3 Franz Kafka, Czech writer, born 1883.

The meaning of life is that it stops.

July

4 Independence Day.

> *Liberty means responsibility.*
> *That is why most men dread it.*
> *—George Bernard Shaw.*

5 Phineas T. Barnum born, 1810.

> *There's a sucker born every minute.*

6 William Faulkner dies, 1962.

> *If a writer has to rob his mother he will not hesitate; the "Ode on a Grecian Urn" is worth any number of old ladies.*

July

7 Sir Arthur Conan Doyle, creator of Sherlock Holmes, dies, 1930.

"What is the meaning of it, Watson?" said Holmes, solemnly, as he laid down the paper. "What object is served by this circle of misery and violence and fear? It must tend to some end, or else our universe is ruled by chance, which is unthinkable. But what end? There is the great problem to which human reason is as far from an answer as ever."

8 John D. Rockefeller born, 1839.

The rich are the scum of the earth in every country.
—G. K. Chesterton.

9 Barbara Cartland, romance novelist, born 1901.

If you want to get rich from writing, write the sort of thing that's read by persons who move their lips when they're reading to themselves.
—Don Marquis.

July

10 Marcel Proust, French novelist, born 1871.

> *I think he was mentally defective.*
> —Evelyn Waugh.

11 E. B. White, American essayist, born 1899.

Our idea of a cultured person is a person who doesn't want to live in a community of cultured persons.

12 Henry David Thoreau born, 1817.

I have lived some thirty years on this planet, and I have yet to hear the first syllable of valuable or even earnest advice from my seniors.

13 Julius Caesar born, 100 B. C.

So long as men worship the Caesars and Napoleons, Caesars and Napoleons will duly rise and make them miserable.
—Aldous Huxley.

July

14 Gerald Ford born, 1913.

> Gerry Ford is a nice guy, but he played too much football with his helmet off.
> —Lyndon B. Johnson.

15 Rembrandt born, 1606.

> That which hears probably more stupidities than anything else in the world is a painting in a museum.
> —Jules de Goncourt.

16 Mary Baker Eddy, founder of Christian Science, dies, 1910.

> A sublime faith in human imbecility has seldom led those who cherish it astray.
> —Havelock Ellis.

17 Art Linkletter (*Kids Say the Darndest Things*), born, 1912.

> I must have been an insufferable child: all children are.
> —G. Bernard Shaw.

July

18 William Makepeace Thackeray, English novelist, born 1811.

Thackeray settled like a meat—fly on whatever one had got for dinner, and made one sick of it.
—John Ruskin.

19 Petrarch, Italian poet, dies, 1374.

We are made to be immortal, and yet we die. It's horrible, it can't be taken seriously.
—Eugene Ionesco.

20 Man lands on the moon, 1969.

The sun and the moon and the stars would have long ago disappeared. . .had they happened to be within the reach of predatory human hands.
—Havelock Ellis.

21 Ernest Hemingway born, 1899.

Always ready to lend a helping hand to the one above him.
—F. Scott Fitzgerald.

July

Robert Burns dies, 1796.

I have a hundred times wished that one could resign life as an officer resigns a commission.

22
Stephen Vincent Benet, poet, born 1898.

We do not fight for the real but for the shadows we make
A flag is a piece of cloth and a word is a sound.

23
Raymond Chandler, American writer, born 1880.

What did it matter where you lay once you were dead? In a dirty sump or in a marble tower on top of a high hill? You were dead, you were sleeping the big sleep, you were not bothered by things like that. Oil and water were the same as wind and air to you.
—The Big Sleep

24
Alexandre Dumas, père, born 1802.

Nobody has read everything of Dumas, not even Dumas himself.
—Anonymous.

July

25 Constitution Day, Puerto Rico.

*When people are free to do as they choose,
they usually imitate each other.*
—Eric Hoffer.

26 George Bernard Shaw born, 1856.

*Life is a disease; and the only difference between one
man and another is the stage of the disease
at which he lives.*

27 Hillaire Belloc, English author, born 1870.

*The moment a man talks to his fellows
he begins to lie.*

28 Gerard Manley Hopkins, English poet, born 1844.

All life death doth end and each day dies with sleep.

July

29 Don Marquis, American humorist, born 1878.

The only obstacle to the progress of the human race is the human race.

30 Emily Bronte, novelist, born 1818.

*Vain are the thousand creeds
That move men's hearts;
unutterably vain;
Worthless as withered weeds,
Or idlest froth amid the boundless main.*

31 First U. S. patent issued, 1790.

Inventor, n. A person who makes an ingenious arrangement of wheels, levers and springs, and believes it civilization.
—Ambrose Bierce.

AUGUST

GET READY FOR THE DOG DAYS!

> *If you pick up a starving dog and make him prosperous, he will not bite you. That is the principal difference between a dog and a man.*
> —Mark Twain

1
Merman Melville (*Moby Dick*), born 1819.

> *Life is a pallid hopelessness.*

2
Warren G. Harding dies, 1923.

> *Harding was not a bad man, he was just a slob.*
> —Alice Roosevelt Longworth.

3
Joseph Conrad, novelist, dies, 1924.

> *About feelings people really know nothing. We talk with indignation or enthusiasm, we talk about oppression, cruelty, crime, devotion, self—sacrifice, virtue, and we know nothing real beyond the words.*

August

4 Percy Bysshe Shelley, poet, born 1792.

*The rapid, blind
And fleeting generations of mankind.*

5 First use of atom bomb, 1945.

*Cursed is every one who placeth his hope in man.
—St. Augustine.*

6 Alfred, Lord Tennyson, born 1809.

What is it all but a trouble of ants in the gleam of a million million of suns?

7 Congress established Order of the Purple Heart, 1782.

*Every hero becomes a bore at last.
—Emerson.*

August

8 Richard Nixon resigns, 1974.

In his private heart no man much respects himself.
—Mark Twain.

9 John Dryden, English poet, born 1631.

Never was a patriot yet, but was a fool.

10 Herbert Hoover born, 1874.

We are in danger in developing a cult of the Common Man, which means a cult of mediocrity.

11

There is many a boy here today who looks on war as all glory, but, boys, it is all hell.
—Speech by Wm. Tecumseh Sherman, Columbus, Ohio, 1880.

August

12 Cecil B. DeMille, movie director, born 1881.

> It is my indignant opinion that 90% of the moving pictures exhibited in America are so vulgar, witless and dull that it is preposterous to write about them in any publication not intended to be
> read while chewing gum.
> —Woolcott Gibbs.

13 Alfred Hitchcock born, 1899.

> Conversation is the enemy of good wine and food.

14 John Galsworthy, English author, born 1867.

> Idealism increases in direct proportion to one's distance from the problem.

15 Thomas DeQuincey, English author, born 1785.

> The peace of nature and of the innocent creatures of God seems to be secure and deep, only so long as the presence of man and his restless and unquiet spirit are not there to trouble its sanctity.

August

16 Elvis Presley dies, 1977.

> To desire immortality is to desire the perpetuation of a great mistake.
> —Arthur Schopenhauer.

17 Mae West born, 1893.

> All wickedness is but little to the wickedness of a woman.
> —Ecclesiastes.

18 Balzac, French writer, dies 1850.

> If we all said to people's faces what we say behind one another's backs, society would be impossible.

19 Ogden Nash born, 1902.

> They take a paper and they read the headlines,
> So they've heard of unemployment and they've heard of breadlines,
> And they philanthropically cure them all
> By getting up a costume charity ball.

August

20 First solo ascent of Mt. Everest, 1980.

Keep you down, and have breakfast while the asinine hunters after the picturesque go braying up the hill.
—William Makepiece Thackeray.

21 American Bar Association founded, 1878.

Lawyers are the only persons in whom ignorance of the law is not punished.
—Jeremy Bentham.

22 Dorothy Parker, American poet and writer, born 1893.

Leave for her a red young rose,
Go your way and save your pity;
She is happy, for she knows
That her dust is very pretty.

23 Gene Kelly, dancer, born 1912.

Dancing? Oh, dreadful. How it is ever adopted in a civilized country I cannot find out.
—Fanny Burney.

August

24 Sir Max Beerbohm, English author, born 1872.

There is always something rather absurd about the past.

25 Bret Harte, American author, born 1836.

He hadn't a sincere fiber in him. I think his heart was merely a pump and had no other function.
—Mark Twain.

26 Women's Equality Day.

Woman may be said to be an inferior man.
—Aristotle.

27 George Hegel, German philosopher, born 1770.

What experience and history teach is this—that people and governments never have learned anything from history.

August

28 Goethe born, 1749.

Man errs, 'till his strife is over.

29 Oliver Wendell Holmes born, 1809.

I see no reason for attributing to man a significant difference in kind from that which belongs to a baboon or a grain of sand.

30 Mary Shelley (Frankenstein), born 1797.

I like a man who talks me to death, provided he is amusing; it saves so much trouble.

31 Itzhak Perlman, violinist, born 1945.

When a man is not disposed to hear musick, there is not a more disagreeable Sound in Harmony than that of a violin.
—Richard Steele.

SEPTEMBER

HOLIDAY OF THE MONTH: Labor Day.

I think there is far too much work done in the world, that immense harm is caused by the belief that work is virtuous.
—Bertrand Russell.

1 World War Two begins, 1939; ends, 1945.

Man: An animal whose chief occupation is extermination of other animals and his own species.
—Ambrose Bierce.

2 Cleveland Amory, American critic, born 1917.

We still say ESP is spinach and stands for Essentially Silly People.

3 e. e. cummings, poet, dies 1962.

To be nobody—but—myself—in a world which is doing its best, night and day, to make you everybody else.

September

4
Chateaubriand, French author and statesman, born 1768.

One is not superior merely because one sees the world in an odious light.

5
Jesse James born, 1841.

Jesse James shot children, but only in fact, not in folklore.
—John Greenway.

6
First Pilgrims set sail for the New World, 1620.

There is no such thing as an American. They are all exiles uprooted, transplanted and doomed to sterility.
—Evelyn Waugh.

7
Queen Elizabeth I born, 1533.

Being a woman is a terribly difficult trade, since it consists primarily of dealing with men.
—Joseph Conrad.

September

8 First U. S. settlement established—St Augustine, Florida—1565.

Cities are the abyss of the human species.
—Rousseau.

9 Leo Tolstoy born, 1828.

History is nothing but a collection of fables and useless trifles, cluttered up with a mass of unnecessary figures and proper names.

10 Cyril Connolly, American critic, born 1903.

What should we think of dogs' monasteries, hermit cats, vegetarian tigers?

11 O'Henry born, 1862.

If men knew how women pass the time when they are alone, they'd never marry.

September

12 H. L. Mencken born, 1880.

My guess is that well over 50 per cent of the human race goes through life without having a single original thought.

13 J. B. Priestley, English novelist and critic, born 1894.

The men who are forever slapping one on the back and saying that everything will come right are bad enough, but more intolerable are those persons who will persist in slapping humanity itself on the back and regarding all life with an unchanging grin of approval.

14 James Fenimore Cooper dies, 1851, one day short of his birthday.

The tendencies of democracies are, in all things, to mediocrity.

September

15 Thomas Wolfe, American novelist, dies, 1938.

Here, then, is man, this moth of time, this dupe of brevity and numbered hours, this travesty of waste and sterile action.

16 Lauren Bacall, American actress, born 1924. Married to Humphrey Bogart.

The whole world is about three drinks behind.
—Bogart.

17 Citizenship Day.

The ideas of the average decently informed person are so warped, and out of perspective, and ignorant, and entirely perverse and wrong and crude. . .that the task of discussing anything with him seriously is simply appalling.
—Arnold Bennett.

September

18 Greta "I vant to be alone" Garbo born, 1905.

> Our life is a sentence of perpetual solitary confinement.
> —Aldous Huxley.

19 William Golding, American author, born 1911.

> Lord of the Flies *was one of the great rip-offs of our time.*
> —Truman Capote.

20 Nothing happened today!

> Hippocleides does not care.
> —Hippocleides.

21 H. G. Wells born, 1866.

Man is a brute. . .a blind prey to impulses. . .victim to endless illusions, which make his mental existence a burden, and fill his life with barren toil and trouble.

September

22 Lord Chesterfield, English statesman, born 1694.

The only solid and lasting peace between a man and his wife is doubtless a separation.

23 Mickey Rooney born, 1920.

The dread of loneliness is greater than the fear of bondage, so we get married.
—Cyril Connolly.

24 F. Scott Fitzgerald born, 1896.

It is in the thirties that we want friends. In the forties we know they won't save us any more than love did.

25 American Indian Day.

America is the only nation in history which miraculously has gone directly from barbarism to degeneration without the usual interval of civilization.
—Georges Clemenceau.

September

26
T. S. Eliot, poet, born 1880.

Human kind cannot bear very much reality.

27
Samuel Adams, American Revolutionary patriot, born 1722.

The 100% American is 99% an idiot.
—*George Bernard Shaw.*

28
Georges Clemenceau, French statesman, born 1841.

Since a politician never believes what he says, he is surprised when others believe him.
—*Charles De Gaulle.*

29
Miguel de Cervantes (*Don Quixote*), born 1547.

Everyone is as God made him, and often a great deal worse.

September

30 Truman Capote, American author, born 1924.

Truman Capote has made lying an art. A minor art.
—Gore Vidal.

OCTOBER

EVENT OF THE MONTH: World Series (sometimes.)

A ball is man's most disastrous invention, not excluding the wheel.
—Robert Morley.

1 World Vegetarian Day.

Health nuts are going to feel stupid someday, lying in hospitals dying of nothing.
—Redd Foxx.

2 Mahatma Gandhi born, 1869.

It is alarming and also nauseating to see Mr. Gandhi...now posing as a fakir of a type well known in the East, striding half-naked up the steps of the viceregal palace!
—Winston Churchill.

3 Thomas Wolfe, American writer, born 1900.

If it must be Thomas let it be Mann, and if it must be Wolfe let it be Nero, but never let it be Thomas Wolfe.
—Peter DeVries.

October

4   St. Francis of Assisi dies, 1226.

> *Saints should always be judged guilty until they are proved innocent.*
> —George Orwell.

---

5   Jonathan Edwards, American religious leader, born 1703.

> *He believed in the worst God, preached the worst sermons, and had the worst religion of any human being who ever lived on this continent.*
> —M. M. Richter.

---

6   Children's Day.

> *All children are essentially criminal.*
> —Diderot.

---

7   Edgar Allan Poe dies, 1849.

> *Epitaph: Quoth the Raven nevermore.*

October

8 Great Chicago Fire, 1871.

(Chicago)...this vicious, stinking zoo...an elegant rockpile monument to everything cruel and stupid and corrupt in the human spirit.
—Hunter S. Thompson.

9 John Lennon born, 1940.

Life is what happens when you are making other plans.

10 Harold Pinter, English playwright, born 1930.

A good many inconveniences attend playgoing in any large cities, but the greatest of these is usually the play itself.
—Kenneth Tynan.

11 François Mauriac, French essayist, born 1885.

What I fear is not being forgotten after my death, but, rather, not being enough forgotten.

October

12 Columbus Day.

> *America is a mistake, a great mistake.*
> *—Sigmund Freud.*

13 Margaret Thatcher, British Prime Minister, born 1925.

> *In general, the art of government consists in taking as much money as possible from one part of the citizens to give it to the other.*
> *—Voltaire.*

14 Dwight D. Eisenhower born, 1890.

> *If all Americans want is security, they can go to prison.*

15 Friedrich Nietzsche, German philosopher, born 1844.

> *An agile but unintelligent and abnormal German, possessed of the mania of grandeur.*
> *—Tolstoy.*

October

16 Eugene O'Neill, playwright, born 1888.

I sometimes think that the United States. . .is the greatest failure the world has ever seen.

17 Evel Knievel born, 1938.

No one ever went broke underestimating the taste of the American public.
—H. L. Mencken.

18 Thomas Love Peacock, English poet and novelist, born 1785.

Respectable means rich, and decent means poor. I should die if I heard my family called decent.

19 Sir Thomas Browne, English physician and author, born 1685.

Man is a noble animal, splendid in ashes, and pompous in the grave.

October

20 John Dewey, American educator, born 1859.

Education: the inculcation of the incomprehensible into the indifferent by the incompetent.
—John Maynard Keynes.

---

21 Alfred Nobel born, 1833. Founded Nobel Prize.

Prizes bring bad luck...(they) encourage hypocrisy.
—Baudelaire.

---

22 Joan Fontaine, American actress, born 1917. Academy Award, 1941.

Nothing would disgust me more, morally, than receiving an Oscar.
—Luis Buñuel.

---

23 Johnny Carson born, 1925.

Talk is cheap because supply exceeds demand.
—Anonymous.

October

24 U. N. Day.

Civilized man is born, lives and dies in slavery; at his birth he is confined in swaddling clothes; at death, he is nailed in a coffin. So long as he retains the human form he is fettered by our institutions.
—Jean Jacques Rousseau.

25 Pablo Picasso born, 1881.

Abstract art: A product of the untalented, sold by the unprincipled to the utterly bewildered.
—Al Capp.

26 Thomas Macaulay, English historian and essayist, born 1800.

The Puritan hated bear-baiting, not because it gave pain to the bear, but because it gave pleasure to the spectators.

27 Dylan Thomas, Irish poet, born 1914.

An alcoholic is someone you don't like who drinks as much as you do.

October

28 Statue of Liberty dedicated, 1886.

You put up in New York Harbor a monstrous idol which you call "Liberty."
—G. B. Shaw.

29 Jean Giradoux, French essayist, born 1882.

Little by little, the pimps have taken over the world. They don't do anything, they don't make anything— they just stand there and take their cut.

30 Richard Sheridan, English dramatist, born 1751.

The newspapers! Sir, they are the most villanous—licentious—abominable—infernal—not that I ever read them— no—I make it a rule never to look into a newspaper.

31 John Keats, poet, born 1795.

I know that poetry is indispensable, but to what?
—Jean Cocteau.

NOVEMBER

HOLIDAY OF THE MONTH: Thanksgiving.

Americans are a race of convicts and ought to be thankful for anything we allow them short of hanging.
—Samuel Johnson.

1 All Saints Day.

Saint, n. A dead sinner revised and edited.
—Ambrose Bierce.

2 George Bernard Shaw dies, 1950.

The world is populated in the main by people who should not exist.

3 André Malraux, French novelist, born 1901.

Men fear silence as they fear solitude, because both give them a glimpse of the terror of life's nothingness.

November

4   Will Rogers born, 1897.

This bosom friend of senators and congressmen was about as daring as an early Shirley Temple movie.
                                            —James Thurber.

5   Election Day.

Politics is perhaps the only profession for which no preparation is thought necessary.
                              —Robert Louis Stevenson.

6   First college football game, 1869.

To watch a football game is to be in prolonged neurotic doubt as to what you're seeing.
                                      —Jacques Barzun.

November

7 Albert Camus born, 1913. (See Jan.4)

*A single sentence will suffice for modern man:
He fornicated and read the papers.*

Billy Graham born, 1918.

*Those who have given themselves the most concern
about the happiness of peoples have made their
neighbors very miserable.*
—Anatole France.

8 Theodore Dreiser's first novel, *Sister Carrie*, published, 1900. He makes $68.40 royalties.

*Life is a God-damned, stinking, treacherous game and
nine hundred and ninety-nine men
out of a thousand are bastards.*

9 This is National Book Week!

*I hate books, for they only teach people to talk about
what they do not understand.*
—Jean Jacques Rousseau.

November

10 Martin Luther born, 1483.

> *No man with any sense of humor
> ever founded a religion.*
> —Robert Ingersoll.

11 Kurt Vonnegut born, 1922.

> *"No wonder kids grow up crazy. A cat's cradle is nothing but a bunch of X's between somebody's hands, and little kids look and look and look at all those X's..."*
>
> *"And?"*
>
> *No damn cat, and no damn cradle."*
> —Cat's Cradle

12 Auguste Rodin, sculptor, born 1840.

> *A fellow will hack half a year at a block of marble to make something in stone that hardly resembles a man.*
> —Samuel Johnson.

November

13 Robert Louis Stevenson born, 1850.

In marriage, a man becomes slack and selfish, and undergoes a fatty degeneration of his moral being.

14 *Moby Dick* published, 1851.

A classic is something that everyone wants to have read and nobody wants to read.
—Mark Twain.

15 Marianne Moore, American poet, born 1887.

The passion for setting people right is in itself an afflictive disease. Distaste which takes no credit to itself is best.

16 George S. Kaufman, American dramatist, born 1889.

The modern theater is a skin disease, a sinful disease of the cities. It must be swept away with a broom.
—Anton Chekhov.

November

17 Marcel Proust, French novelist, dies, 1922.

Do not the indiscretions which occur only after a person's life on earth is ended prove that nobody really believes in a future life?

18 W. S. Gilbert, English librettist, born 1836.

Man is nature's sole mistake.

19 Lincoln's Gettysburg Address, 1863.

Democracy means simply the bludgeoning of the people by the people for the people.
—Oscar Wilde.

20 Leo Tolstoy dies, 1910.

The meaningless absurdity of life is the only incontestable knowledge known to man.

November

21 Voltaire born, 1694.

Men will always be mad and those who think they can cure them are the maddest of all.

22 George Gissing, English novelist, born 1857.

It is because nations tend to stupidity and baseness that mankind moves so slowly.

23 Harpo Marx born, 1893.

It is a far, far better thing to have a firm anchor in nonsense than to put out on the troubled seas of thought.
—J. K. Galbraith.

24 Dale Carnegie (author of *How To Win Friends and Influence People*), born 1888.

The ability to deal with people is as purchasable a commodity as sugar or coffee.
—John D. Rockefeller.

November

25 Andrew Carnegie, American manufacturer and philanthropist, born 1835.

The rich get richer and the poor get poorer.

26 Charles ("Peanuts") Schulz born, 1922.

I have a new philosophy. I'm only going to dread one day at a time.
   —Charlie Brown.

27 Eugene O'Neill, playwright, dies 1953.

*None of us can help the things life has
   done to us. . .
Everything comes between you and what
you'd
   like to be,
and you have lost your true self forever.*

28 First broadcast of Grand Ole Opry, 1925.

Music is essentially useless, as life is.
   —George Santayana.

November

29 Louisa May Alcott (*Little Women*), born 1832.

Literature is the orchestration of platitudes.
—Thornton Wilder.

30 Mark Twain born, 1835.

There are times one would like to hang the whole human race, and finish the farce.

DECEMBER

HOLIDAY OF THE MONTH: Christmas

If Jesus Christ were to come today, people would not even crucify him. They would ask him to dinner, hear what he had to say, and make fun of him.
—Thomas Carlyle.

1 Woody Allen born, 1935.

If my film makes one more person miserable, I feel I've done my job.

2 Marquis de Sade dies, 1814.

I never wonder to see men wicked, but I often wonder to see them not ashamed.

3 Joseph Conrad, Polish writer, born 1857.

The belief in a supernatural source of evil is not necessary; men alone are quite capable of every wickedness.

December

4 Samuel Butler, English writer, born 1835.

Life is one long process of getting tired.

5 Prohibition repealed, 1933.

Alcohol is the anaesthesia by which we endure the operation of life.
—G. B. Shaw.

6 Joyce Kilmer, poet, born 1886.

"Trees," if I have the name right, is one of the most annoying pieces of verse within my knowledge.
—Heywood C. Broun.

7 Willa Cather, American novelist, born 1873.

I don't care how well she writes; I don't give a damn what people in Nebraska do.
—H. L. Mencken.

8 James Thurber born, 1894.

Sixty minutes of thinking of any kind is bound to lead to confusion and unhappiness.

9 John Milton born, 1608.

Poetry's unnat'ral; no man ever talked poetry 'cept a beadle on boxin' day.
—Charles Dickens.

10 Emily Dickinson born, 1830.

It is essential to the sanity of mankind that each one should think the other crazy.

December

11 Alexander Solzhenitsyn, Russian writer, born 1918.

Freedom! To spit in the eye and in the soul of the passerby and the passenger with advertising!
—Solzhenitsyn

He is a bad novelist and a fool. The combination usually makes for great popularity in the U. S.
—Gore Vidal.

12 First trans-Atlantic radio signal transmitted, 1901.

The gift of broadcasting is, without question, the lowest human capacity to which any man could attain.
—Harold Nicolson.

13 Samuel Johnson, English writer, dies 1784.

The goal of all life is death.
—Freud.

December

14 South Pole discovered, 1911.

Great God! this is an awful place.
—Robert F. Scott, Polar explorer.

15 Izaak Walton, famous fisherman, dies 1683.

Angling or float fishing I can only compare to a stick
and a string, with a worm at one end
and a fool at the other.
—Samuel Johnson.

16 Jane Austen, writer, born 1775.

Why do we live? But to make sport for our neighbors
and laugh at them in return.

17 Wright Brothers Day.

The conquest of the air. . .may turn out to be the most
sinister event that ever befell us.
—John Galsworthy.

December

18 Francis Thompson, poet, born 1859.

*Nothing begins and nothing ends
That is not paid with moan
For we are born in other's pain
And perish in our own.*

19 Emily Bronte, English novelist, dies, 1848.

It (writing) is the most ignoble of professions.
—Gustave Flaubert.

20 John Steinbeck dies, 1968.

I can't read ten pages of Steinbeck without throwing up.
—James Gould Cozzens.

21 Winter begins.

Winter changes into stone the water of heaven and the heart of man.
—Victor Hugo.

December

22 Edward Arlington Robinson, American poet, born 1869.

The popular interpretation of Christianity makes me sick.

23 NBC establishes coast-to-coast radio network, 1928.

Radio is a bag of mediocrity where little men with carbon minds wallow in sluice of their own making.
—Fred Allen.

24 Christmas Eve. Matthew Arnold, English poet and critic, born 1822.

Miracles do not happen.

December

25 Christmas Day.

...Several hundred million people get a billion or so gifts for which they have no use, and some thousands of shop-clerks die of exhaustion while selling them and every other child in the western world is made ill from overeating—all in the name of the lowly Jesus.
—Upton Sinclair.

26

I never could see why people were so happy about Dickens' "A Christmas Carol" because I never had any confidence that Scrooge was going to be different the next day.
—Dr. Karl Menninger.

27 Charles Lamb, English essayist, dies, 1834.

My theory is to enjoy life, but the practice is against it.

December

28 Pledge of Allegiance sanctioned by Congress, 1945.

> Nothing like a solemn oath.
> People always think you mean it.
> —Norman Douglas.

---

29 Wounded Knee massacre, 1890.

> He (the Indian) is ignoble—base and treacherous, and hateful in every way. Not even imminent death can startle him into a spasm of virtue.
> —Mark Twain.

---

30 Rudyard Kipling born, 1865.

> Lo, all our pomp of yesterday
> Is one with Nineveh and Tyre!

---

31 New Year's Eve. A new year starts tomorrow!

> Taken as a whole, the universe is absurd.
> —Walter Savage Landor.